the SUPER Simple guide to

WATERFALLS & FOUNTAINS

for Your Garden Pond

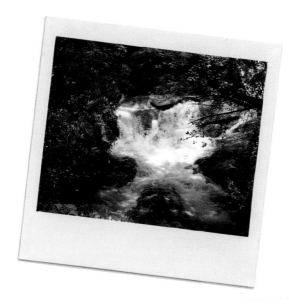

Terry Anne Barber

D1706374

t.f.h.

T.F.H. Publications, Inc.

© 2003 T.F.H. Publications, Inc.

Distributed in the UNITED STATES to the Pet Trade by T.F.H. Publications, Inc., 1 TFH Plaza, Neptune City, NJ 07753; on the Internet at www.tfh.com; in CANADA by Rolf C. Hagen Inc., 3225 Sartelon St., Montreal, Quebec H4R 1E8; Pet Trade by H & L Pet Supplies Inc., 27 Kingston Crescent, Kitchener, Ontario N2B 2T6; in ENGLAND by T.F.H. Publications, PO Box 74, Havant PO9 5TT; in AUSTRALIA AND THE SOUTH PACIFIC by T.F.H. (Australia), Pty. Ltd., Box 149, Brookvale 2100 N.S.W., Australia; in NEW ZEALAND by Brooklands Aquarium Ltd., 5 McGiven Drive, New Plymouth, RD1 New Zealand; in SOUTH AFRICA by Rolf C. Hagen S.A. (PTY.) LTD., P.O. Box 201199, Durban North 4016, South Africa; in Japan by T.F.H. Publications. Published by T.F.H. Publications, Inc.

Library of Congress Cataloging-in-Publication Data
Barber, Terry Anne.
The super simple guide to waterfalls & fountains / Terry Anne Barber.
p. cm.
1. Water gardens. 2. Fountains. I. Title.
SB423 .B27 2003
714--dc22
2003017194

Contents

Lots of
Supplies
Page 46

Chapter 5 - Installing the Hidden Sump Fountain 53

Chapter 6 - Installing a Wall Fountain 65

Part One
Fantastic Fountains

"Honey, I know you're just trying to please, but this isn't what I had in mind when I asked for a garden fountain."

Introduction to Fountains

The fountain is a very old fixture of human civilization, though the humble beginnings of the fountain were purely functional. A fountain was a place for people and animals to get clean drinking water, and the first ones were built to enclose springs. Later, people learned how to channel water to their settlements, but the town

A Hydria-A ceramic pot used by the women of ancient Greece to carry water from fountains.

fountain was still important. As technology grew, the fountain became more than just a place to get a drink.

Water has a great importance in most religions, often being used to wash away sins. Water symbolizes life and birth and it can be calm or uncontrollable. We feel a connection to water. Using water in artistic expression can convey many emotions by adding sound and movement to the viewing experience.

Historical Fountains

Fountains have been a part of the human experience since ancient times. The ancient Greeks built columnar shrines over springs and dedicated them to deities or nymphs. The necessity of water to a community certainly made clean drinking water something to celebrate and consider a gift of the gods. Greek women would collect water from the local spring each day as part of the housekeeping chores.

Fountains add a touch of formality to corporate parks and campuses.

In ancient Rome, much of the required water was taken from the Tiber River. Natural springs also existed, which would have utilitarian fountains built around them to make them easier to use. Aqueducts were used to bring water to Imperial Rome to provide water for the city's large population. The estates of the wealthy had their own baths and fountains, while public fountains supplied the community at large. There are even the remains of a fountain inside the Coloseum.

Fountain building was a favorite hobby of the wealthy throughout Europe in the 16th and 17th centuries, and a fountain-building boom took place during this time. In Italy, many fountains were built in the Renaissance period and beyond, and presently, there are more than 280 fountains in Rome alone. One of the most famous fountains ever built in Rome is the Trevi Fountain. The Trevi Fountain was constructed over a 100-year time span and was completed in the late 1700s. Neptune, a popular figure for fountains, is boldly featured in this fountain. Legend says that if you throw a coin over your shoulder into Trevi Fountain, you will guarantee your eventual return to Rome.

Large formal fountains can also be used to accent apartment complexes.

Another example is the French Palace of Versailles, which still has many of its original fountains and

Need head

Small fountains in particular have become very popular for home yards and gardens. You will be able to find a fountain that fits your budget and will look great in your landscape, too.

pools. These were built so well that very little work has been needed to keep these water features in working condition. The source for the Palace's water was a constant worry for Louis the XIV, and to help remedy the concern, a reservoir 500 feet above the palace was constructed to power all of the water displays.

In Salzburg, Austria, Archbishop Markus Sitticus put his odd sense of humor to good use by designing Hellbrunn Castle with a variety of fountains and water gags. One of these water tricks was a dining table that would douse the guests with water upon the Archbishop's signal. In Spain, Moorish fountains were usually a basin combined with sculpture; the Fountain of the Lions in the Alhambra, Granada, is the most famous. You can visit most of these grand fountains today while touring Europe.

The Europeans were certainly not the only ones to build fountains. Fountains in Islamic countries often emit an inconspicuous trickle instead of gushing water. In gardens, there may be a small spray of water rising from the middle of a quiet pool filled with water lilies. Public fountains in Middle Eastern cities are entirely enclosed within structures. You can see examples in Istanbul, Cairo, and Damascus.

Modern Times

Like they say, history repeats itself. The fountain builders of today often incorporate features of older fountain styles with new ideas to construct the contemporary looks of modern times. The key is to keep the fountain efficient without losing the desired look you want to ultimately portray. You may have seen some of these modern types of fountains in familiar places you have visited or vacationed. Some of these may pulse water in changing patterns or in patterns

Children often love to play in modern fountains.

that are synchronized to music. Some are even incorporated in a show where the fountains are only part of the display. The use of valves and pumps that are controlled by computers can produce spectacular results. The closing display at Epcot Center in Orlando, Florida and the Fountain of Bellagio in Las Vegas, Nevada are outstanding examples of computer-controlled fountain displays.

Is a Fountain a Water Garden?

A fountain can be easily added to an existing water garden and even to a large pond or lake, but we do not consider them as water gardens in the traditional sense. If you are keeping fish, a fountain is an excellent way to aerate your garden pond. You can buy a variety of fountain kits that are appropriate for all sizes of pools and water gardens.

A popular design for a fountain includes a pool with a water spray and may include statues. Many of the ancient fountains we talked about, such as the Middle Eastern types, traditionally contained fish and water lilies. However, many fountain styles would not provide a good home to fish or water plants. They could be too small or not provide enough water to sustain life. For example, a multi-tiered fountain would not make a good water garden because they often have very shallow dishes where the water overflows into the next tier.

Many people use fountains to enhance the look of a water garden.

The basin, or the bottom tier, on the other hand, will usually provide a deep enough water level to allow the growth of some emergent vegetation such as cattails, iris, or pickerel rush. Along with these plants, you may be able to house small fish such as mosquito fish, *Gambusia* spp., or other live-bearing fishes like guppies, *Poecillia* spp. The addition of these fishes to any outside water feature is important in controlling the presence of pest insects.

To Fountain or Not to Fountain

What do fountains offer today's homeowner? A fountain in your garden or yard has many benefits, and it is certainly something interesting to add to your landscape. Fountains provide a source of sound and movement in the garden. The sound of running or trickling water is soothing. We all could use a private retreat to soothe us after a hard day at the office or with the kids. The wide variety of styles guarantees that you will find a style and size that will suit you.

Not all fountains need to put out large volumes of water to be effective.

A Fountain Style For Everyone

Going Formal

The word formal probably brings to mind images of floating around the dance floor in a luxurious mansion, wearing a gown or tuxedo. Now just swirl yourself over through the door to the patio or balcony, and take a good look. You bet there is a formal fountain out there!

Formal pool and fountain at the Atlanta Botanical Gardens.

Okay, so that was a bit much, but some buildings and gardens are well suited to a more formal approach. A formal water garden is the centerpiece to a more complex landscape. For example, corporate offices often contain formal water gardens in their lobbies. These water gardens do not have to be large; in fact, many are rather small. It is not the size of the pond that classifies it as "formal;" it is the pond's appearance.

Formal garden ponds can be designated by several things; the use of pavers for pathways around or leading up to the pond, a bench to provide a sitting place overlooking the pond, and a flat-stone border encircling the water line of the pond are all important features to the design of a formal water garden. Formal water gardens should appear as if they were built using materials that were precisely measured and formed together for a perfect fit on all sides.

The formal water garden must contain a formal water fountain and can have geometric or classical shapes. Round is most common; however, square, rectangular, and other polygons give you some more shapes to choose from. The formal fountain should closely match the appearance of the water garden it is situated in. There are several components of formal fountains that you can choose either entirely or just in pieces.

The Formal Pool

A very beautiful and simple way to build a fountain is to build a formal-shaped pool and add a spray or bubbler in the center.

Centering the spray is important in maintaining the formality of the design, but the pool itself can be of many shapes and styles. This type of fountain can be thought of more as a water garden with a fountain added. The pool itself will be the main attraction, while the fountain is the icing on the cake. There are many ways you can construct this type of design, so choose the best one that suits you both in function and monetary expense.

This spray nozzle adds air to the water to give it a foamy effect.

The pool can be set in the ground, above the ground, or halfway between. All but the smallest pondfish need a pool that is at least 2 feet deep, but many water plants will do just fine in a more shallow pool. Formal pools are becoming increasingly popular as additions to decks and patios and are often used to give a dead corner some much-needed life.

A structured edging gives a formal design a polished look and ties the design together. Many materials can be used to finish the edging of the pool. Brick or other masonry blocks work well. For a

A series of spray jets turns this pool into a fountain.

A small fountain will help aerate the water, especially in the summer.

sunken pool, slate or tile allows you to precisely craft the edges. If you are really adventurous, you can try going for a Middle Eastern design and create a pool that is edged in small tiles or a mosaic design.

Adding a Fountain Spray

Now you simply build on the pool design and add a fountain spray to the center of the pool. First you need to find the center of the pool, which should be fairly simple because you used a geometric design. You only need a few tools to find your center; a pencil, a measuring tape, some twine, and some duct tape.

Use your measuring tape to find the center point on each side of the pool and make a small mark with your pencil. A 5-foot wide by 7-foot long pool will have centers at 2.5 feet and 3.5 feet respectively. Now you just draw the twine across the top of the pool at each center and the point where the two pieces meet is the center of the pool. You could drop a stone or some other marker into the water to "hold" the place for you, or just directly place the fountain in.

If you have a circular shaped pool or an irregular shape, the procedure is very similar. Simply take four sections of wood (like 2 X 4s) that would completely surround the pond, making a perfect square around it. Now you are able to use the method for measuring formal ponds to find the perfect center of the pond.

This angel offers the birds a drink.

Another complicated factor is making your fountain level. You may need to create a stable base to place your small fountain, and doing so will often require you to get in your pond to get it positioned and leveled just right. Upside-down flowerpots, plastic milk crates, or stones are all good platforms. You can level your platform by using the plastic shims that you can find at a home improvement store. Cement blocks will probably raise the pH of your water. I don't think this will cause any harm, but you should be aware of this possibility.

A Potential Pitfall

The pump-fountain combinations are very nice in this application, but most of them also have a foam filter attached to the pump inlet. This isn't a bad idea, but you won't like climbing out to the middle of your pond to take it out and clean it when it eventually clogs. You can try running it with the sponge in place. If your water is very clear, it won't clog. If it does clog quickly, try leaving it off.

Look for a statue of Neptune if you are going for a classic look. Neptune was often the subject of choice for fountains because he is the Roman god of water. Today, animals, angels, and children are the most prevalent subjects for ready-made fountains.

A classic statue gives this fountain a formal and classy look. Wakoola Water gardens.

Spray Patterns

Unless you have a really large pool, my advice is to purchase an off-the-shelf pump and spray fountain combination. Many manufacturers offer spray fountains with matched nozzles and pumps to create the right look for your pool. You will be able to find them with adjustable spray patterns or only one pattern. The following are some of the pump and spray patterns that are available for your fountain:

• **Bubblers or foaming sprays:** mix

air with water and will not go too high in the air.

• **Bell-shaped sprays:** make an upside-down, bowl shaped display.

• **Tulip-shaped patterns:** spray up with one or more levels of circular falling water patterns.

• **Spitters:** are just little fountains. They are usually animals and the water comes out of the animal's mouth.

Create Your Own

What if you find the perfect statue to use as a fountain, but the statue was not meant to be a fountain in the first place? There are two ways to incorporate your statue into your fountain setup. First, it may look just as nice as a statue near your pond or even in the pond. You could build a pedestal for Neptune in the middle of your pond and let him be a dry watcher of the fishes.

Another solution is to convert the statue into a fountain or a spitter. It all depends on the way they are made and your determination. A good example is a terra cotta fish statue that I have. The fish is hollow, making it ideal for conversion to a fountain. Then all I would have to do is place some flexible aquarium tubing inside the fish and position it strategically to make a spray come out of the fish's mouth. With this fish, I could also use a fountain nozzle for the pattern of my choice. I would need to use some silicone RTV to glue the tubing in place. If you choose this method, make sure you use aquarium grade silicone that is non-toxic to the critters in your pond or pool.

A gnome adds a bit of whimsical spitting into this container water garden.

Choosing the Right Pump

If you are not buying a fountain and pump combo, then how would you know which pump to buy for your homemade fountain? This can be a dilemma, but you don't have to worry about getting bogged down in some nasty engineering calculations. A good rule of thumb for a fountain with a smooth bore nozzle (like tubing) is to get a pump with a head of 1.2 times the desired height of the stream. If the pump has a max head pressure of 5 feet (the box will tell you this number), the height of the stream would be 5 divided by 1.2 or about 4.2 feet. Another thing to keep in mind is that you can restrict the opening of the pump and this will give the water a greater velocity.

The Informal Pool

Most people probably prefer a more informal pool or garden pond. There are many ways to build an informal pool using liners, preformed ponds, and even small containers. The informal pool will usually have a more natural looking form and finish. The pool will use relaxed curves and blend into the surrounding landscape. Mulch, rocks, and turf are all good choices for finishing the edge of a natural pool. The pool could also be raised with wooden ties or stone for the edge.

Everything that we discussed already about formal pools can be applied to the informal pool. Just relax some of the rules. For example, don't worry about placing the fountain in the center of the pool. Of course you can estimate the "middle" and place it there, but you can also just go with what looks good to you. In addition, your choice of fountain or spitter can be a classic form (like that statue of Neptune) or something more eclectic. Even a pink flamingo might work for your informal pool.

Pep up Your Pool with a Statue

A very classic design is to place a statue in the pool and spray water up from the pool onto the statue. You could place several sprays around the fountain to give a more dramatic result.

You may also decide to go with a statue that becomes the fountain. The variety and availability of statuary has really increased. You will even find many statues, large and small, which have already been designed to work as a fountain.

Modern Art

What picture does the words modern art conjure up in your imagination? Do you think of paintings by Picasso? Do you think of the splashes of Jackson Pollack? How about the sculpture of Alexander Calder? Lot's of things have been called modern art. Some aren't modern and some may not be art, but you can use these styles in your fountain.

Modern styles usually include geometric shapes. Go back to your formal pool as a base. Update the edging to a crisply cut stone or unusual materials, such as metal and you are off to a good start. Here is where a sculpture can really bring your pool to life. A bold, modern statue can be used in a pool, beside a pool, or as a stand-alone fountain. Here your imagination is the limit.

Asian Influence

Fancy goldfish and koi originate from Asia, and a Chinese or Japanese style pond is a great way to display these beautiful fish. You won't find a dramatic spray of water or gushing fountain in an Asian-influenced garden; these styles are based on tranquility and reflection.

A large alligator spitter guards this water garden.

The royal palaces in China had gardens covering hundreds of acres. The idea was to mimic the Chinese landscape in a compact form in these gardens. Woods, hills, streams, and ponds were all part of the garden. The garden became a way to display wealth in China. Families sought to emulate the emperor and create smaller scale gardens on their property and still incorporate all of these design elements. One interesting aspect of the Chinese garden is the attempt to capture the essence of mountains with elaborate rockwork.

Part 1

Fountains with Chinese design have become popular with the current Feng Shui method. Feng Shui is the art of object placement. The goal is to arrange your environment to bring you balance. Water balances wind–literally translated Feng is wind and Shui is water. Therefore, small fountains are part of the design. The form requires study and there are many good books out there if you really want to use this style.

The art of gardening in Japan differs from the Chinese approach. Though early Japanese gardens were a direct reflection of the Chinese form, the arrival of Zen Buddhism from China via Korea in the sixth century changed garden design in Japan. The ideas of emulating nature remained, but the emphasis was on simplicity.

Because the emphasis in an Asian garden is tranquility and nature, a fountain may not even be authentic in an Asian garden. That doesn't mean that you can't include one, however. Use you imagination and some of the style ideas we have already talked about to create your own vision. How about an Asian statue as the focal point of a fountain? There is no reason not to invent your own image.

Here, a fish spitter adds interest to the edge of large pond.

A small fountain dresses up this informal garden pond. Wakoola Water gardens.

There are a few items that you can find traditionally associated with a Japanese water garden. One of these is the deer chaser, which uses a small stream to fill a stalk of bamboo. The stalk fills, then tips over and bangs on a rock. Many pond or garden suppliers have deer chasers ready-made, but they are very easy to make yourself.

Finally, an interesting item to accent your Japanese-style garden is a tsukubai (crouching basin). The Tea Ceremony is a ritual that is closely associated with Zen Buddhism and incorporates the Zen ideals of Harmony, Respect, Purity, and Tranquility. A tsukubai is a stone water basin that traditionally is placed next to a teahouse. As guests emerge from the garden and arrive at the teahouse, the ceremony required that they perform the ritual of washing their hands and rinsing their mouths using a simple bamboo dipper and water from the tsukubai. The water was either added to the basin before the guest arrived or was provided by a continuously flowing fountain called a kakei. A tsukubai can become a real conversation piece in your garden.

Searching for Fountains

Garden fountains have become so popular that you won't have a difficult time finding them. Most garden centers and large retailers with garden sections are carrying a good selection. If you ever want to find something unusual or made of superior materials, however, you may have to hunt.

I have found some really wonderful granite garden fountains in out-of-the-way, roadside garden centers. Keep your eyes open as you travel around and you may find a gem. But what if you don't want to wander around the countryside seeking that perfect fountain? Hit the Internet. There are some really amazing and high-quality statuary and fountains being advertised via the web. Use your favorite search engine and happy hunting.

Making Preparations

Utilizing Utilities

Your fountain will need water and electricity nearby to bring it to life. Water will be the easy one to provide. Since your fountain will be filled, cleaned, and topped up occasionally, you don't need to have a permanent connection to water. The garden hose will work just fine; just get a hose that is long enough to reach the

Bamboo can add style to any water feature.

Always use a GFIC when using electrical devices in and around water. It could save your life.

A ground fault circuit interrupter.

Reset
Test

fountain. A good spray nozzle will come in handy for cleaning, too.

Safety Please!

Water is a very good electrical conductor, and it is unsafe to mix water and electricity.

Because of this potential danger, there are nationwide building codes specific to areas of the home where water and electricity can come into contact. For example, it is now code to have a Ground Fault Interruption Circuit (GFIC) in bathrooms and garages. In your household wiring, electricity flows into an appliance and back out again. The GFIC has its own circuit that measures the current going out and coming back. If there is a failure to ground (in other words, the electricity doesn't come back), it shuts off the circuit.

GFICs can be purchased in many forms. The least expensive and most readily available is a replacement for your household electrical plug. It has a little red button for testing and also a reset button. It is a very good idea to test the circuit once in a while to make sure it is working. You just push the red button and it should turn off the socket. A good time to test the GFIC is just before you plan to work around your pond.

GFICs can also be purchased as part of an extension cord. These are a little more expensive but are well worth the cost. Many folks have an extension cord running out to their pond, and this is a great way to use a GFIC. Most home improvement stores will carry both the plug and the extension cord types of GFIC.

There are also building codes regarding the proximity of electrical outlets to swimming pools. A distance of 15 feet from the pool is required by building codes in most states. Please check up on your local building codes. Use swimming pools as your guideline and remember to always use caution.

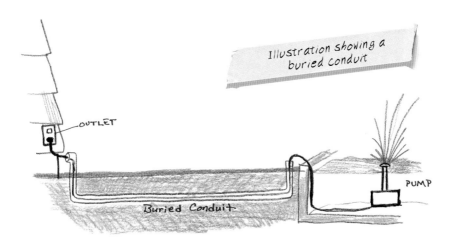

Illustration showing a buried conduit

OUTLET

PUMP

Buried Conduit

Getting Power to the Fountain

Now that we have the safety lecture out of the way, how can you power the pump for your fountain? A bright orange electrical cord snaking across the lawn just wouldn't add to the design. If you want a permanently installed electrical line to your fountain, it may be best to call an electrician and have them install a line to the fountain. My suggestion would be to have them install this line in an underground conduit to the location and have a waterproof receptacle at the site. Make sure they use a GFIC for your safety.

Depending on the location of your fountain, you may be able to get away with an outdoor extension cord. Most outlets placed on the exterior of your home will have a GFIC built in, so you won't need to buy one included with the electrical cord. If the fountain is very close to the house, just use mulch or other natural landscaping materials to cover the cord.

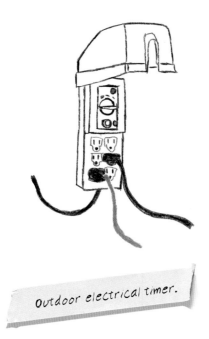

Outdoor electrical timer.

Time Out

I also recommend that you install a timer for your fountain. In most cases, the fountain will not be viewed at night, so why not turn it off and save the power? The timer will save at least half of the electric bill of running the fountain. In very dry climates, such as the desert southwest, you should turn your fountain off at night so you can save on water evaporation. The longer the water spends exposed to air, the more evaporation you will experience.

Look for a timer for outdoor use. An indoor timer may work, but if it gets wet, it will probably quit on you. Look for them at home improvement stores and other large retailers. If they don't carry what you want, then try garden centers that specialize in the sales and installation of water gardens and fountains. Be careful––many outdoor timers are designed to turn on holiday lights or other outdoor lighting. That means they only turn on at night, just the opposite of what you may want for your fountain.

Light it Up

If you are like me, you are a night owl and like to see your fountain in the evening. Why not add some lights? Outdoor spots can highlight your fountain from above or below. Pond-supply outlets will also carry waterproof lights that can go inside the water. These lights come with colored lenses that allow you to change them as the seasons change or for different holidays and so on.

Misters

Another cool gadget you can use in your fountain is a sonic mister. They sit just under the surface of the water and create a foggy mist above the surface. When used in conjunction with colored lenses, misters can create an eerie-colored mist flowing over the edge of the fountain. Use caution with misters. They produce high levels of carbon dioxide, which can kill your fish. As long as you have good surface movement, you should have no problems with misters, but always keep that precaution in the back of your mind.

Pump it Up!

There is a science behind choosing the correct pump for a fountain. The requirements for a fountain pump will be less rigorous than for a waterfall, but you still need to be up to speed on the idea of pump head and head loss. Head is the height that you want the pump to push the water. Head loss is the friction loss due to the piping along the way. If the top of your fountain is 5 feet up, the pump needs to get the water at least that high, preferably much higher.

A common style water pump.

Unless you are building a really huge fountain, you will almost always be using a centrifugal submersible pump. Submersible pumps will go right down into the center of the fountain and make things much more simple. They usually have an extra long cord that comes in handy, especially with fountains.

Flow Rate

Fountain and pump combinations already have the pump selected for you. If the pump is not packaged with the fountain you like, use a pump with a flow rate of half the pond volume per hour. For example, if your small pond is 200 gallons, use a pump that is rated at a 100 gallon per hour flow rate.

Because fountain nozzles would require you to do some really nasty calculations, just ask the manufacturer—-they have already done the hard work for you. Tell them you need to know the flow and head needed for the nozzle. Also ask for the height the water will rise from the

Selecting a Pump

The steps to selecting a pump for a fountain are as follows.

1. Determine the flow rate needed.

2. Determine the system head loss.

3. Pick a pump.

Pump, plumbing, and filter kit for a large pond.

nozzle at different conditions of head and flow. Simply select a pump that will provide the desired flow/head combo. Keep the height of the spray to one half the diameter of your pond or basin to prevent excessive water loss.

Tiered fountains and overflowing containers will require a little work from you, but these calculations are relatively easy. You just need to calculate the inches of fountain rim for the largest tier that will have water flowing over it. For an overflowing container, that would be the rim of the vessel. Here is the formula:

Flow Rate gal/hour = Inches x 50 gal/inch/hour

Let's work it out for a three-tiered fountain where the largest tier (careful, don't use the bottom one because the water doesn't flow over it!) is 18 inches in diameter. Remember the formula for finding the circumference of a circle?

Circumference = Diameter x Π (pi, or 3.14)

The fountain must be level, or the water will flow or spray off in odd directions.

If you apply this formula to the fountain where the largest tier is 18 inches in diameter, the equation would be as follows:

18 x 3.14 = 56 inches x 50 gal/inch/hour = 2800 gallons per hour.

Wow! That is a very high flow rate for most conventional water features. Careful inspection of the fountain may result in finding the fountain is fluted. In this case, the distance the water falls is 5 inches, so the required flow rate would be greatly lessened to 250 gallons per hour.

For this reason, you need to be very careful when choosing the appropriate flow rate for your fountain, as the waterfall formula may be misleading. There is an old saying that similarly applies here: measure twice, cut once. The pump's box will normally indicate what the suggested application is by the manufacturer.

Roughing It

The amount of flow that gives your fountain a pleasant display is somewhat a matter of taste. Maybe you are the pleasant trickle type or the macho mega spray man. Simply choose a pump that is a little larger than recommended. This will let you adjust the flow to the pond. Use a pinch clamp on the tubing or small ball valve to adjust the flow.

There are many types of rock available to choose from in order to customize your project.

Another way to make a rough estimate of the pump size is to

buy your fountain before you purchase the pump. Set up the fountain; then connect it to your garden hose. Adjust the flow of the garden hose until you get a flow rate that looks good to you. Don't touch the flow rate that you set on the hose. Disconnect the hose from the fountain, and then measure the length of time it takes to fill a 5-gallon bucket. Now you know an approximate flow rate, you know the height of the fountain (the head). Just look for a pump that will match.

Supporting Materials

When working out your budget, save some cash for the supporting landscape materials that you will need to complete your design and firmly support your fountain. Rockwork, gravel, sand, mulch, and bricks are all possible materials that you may want to use.

An underwater light is used for accenting certain features.

The good news is that most home improvement stores and garden centers are carrying a wider variety of hardscape materials than ever. You can find stones and gravel of many colors to work with. Pavers make great base materials for a stand-alone fountain. Shop around for the items that will coordinate with your new fountain.

Bigger projects will require larger quantities of finishing materials. Buying gravel in 25-pound bags would get expensive quickly. Your home improvement center or nursery may be able to provide materials by the truckload to you. I have found that an inexpensive way to buy gravel and rock is to find the nearest quarry. They will be able to offer gravel and rock in many sizes. Ask them to recommend a trucking company to deliver for you. The only drawback to local material is that is may not be the color you want.

Installing a Classic Tiered Fountain

The tiered fountain is a classic design and adds an air of formality to any landscape. You can place the tiered fountain as a stand-alone or in a matching basin. Look for a basin that matches the style of your tiered fountain. Let's go through the steps that it will take to install your new fountain and make it look great.

Antique style three-tiered fountain. Wakoola Watergardens.

The Ace of Base

Of all the fountain types we have discussed, this style will be very intolerant of an unleveled base. If a tier is slightly uneven, you will see more water flow from one side than the others. Your goal is to have the water flow evenly all around the tier. Therefore, leveling will be much of the work of the installation.

The most important place to start is the base. There are many ways to provide a base that will work well for your tiered fountain.

Don't forget the electricity. Have your electrical hook up installed before or during the process of building your base. It would really be a pain to forget and then have to dig something up to bury the electrical line.

This base is ready to move into position.

Things You Will Need:

1. Fountain
2. Pump
3. Tubing matched to pump outlet
4. Tubing clamp to adjust flow rate
5. Electricity source to site
6. Sand and finish rock
7. Cement mix, Cinder blocks and/or bricks as needed
8. Tools - shovel, level, razor knife, tubing cutter, silicone RTV

Pour It

For a small base that would fit great in a garden or flowerbed you should use poured concrete. Dig a hole that is a little larger in diameter than the diameter of the base of your fountain. Most home improvement stores have cardboard forms that can be placed in the hole to give you a nice circular base. Mix up concrete using the package instructions and fill the hole. Carefully finish the top surface of the concrete to make it smooth and level. Use a bubble level to insure that the top is level. You can cover any exposed concrete with mulch or even dirt to blend in with the surroundings.

A formal tiered fountain placed in a flowerbed is a mixed style. You can keep it a little more informal by not using a basin.

Pave It

A second base that works well and looks more formal is to use pavers or bricks. I'll briefly review the steps, but you can also find several "How-To" books on building a patio floor with pavers or bricks. First excavate the area to the depth of the paver plus four inches. You should make this area as level as possible as you excavate.

The bottom tier is placed on the base first, as shown here.

Part 1

You will need masonry sand to create a firm under layer. I like to use lumber to help level and compact the sand in the under layer. First build a frame with 2x4s that sets down in the excavation. Use your bubble level to get the frame as level as possible. Then fill the frame with sand and compact it. Finally scrape another 2x4 across the top of the frame. This will help you to notice any areas that are lower than others and allow you to level them off.

The next step is to place the pavers or bricks. A string stretched across your work area will help you place them level. You can even buy a small bubble level that attaches to the string so you can find level. Tap each brick or paver into place with a rubber mallet. Keep working and soon you will have a great looking platform. Finally, brush sand into the crevices between the pavers. The sand will act as a spacer and will help prevent the bricks from moving around when you walk on them.

The tubing has been connected to the pump and pulled through

Placin' Basin

If you choose to use a basin for your tiered fountain, you may find that leveling the tiers will be easier. I am assuming that you have purchased a preformed basin and are not building your own. Its not a problem if you build your own; just make the bottom as perfectly level as possible.

If you decide to place the basin on the ground, use my "excavate and sand" method mentioned above to create a level base. Be fussy about it. Put the basin down and test it for levelness. Add some more sand where you need it. Do it all over again. The more level the basin, the better the end result.

The tubing is threaded through the second basin.

Adding Tiers

Start from the bottom and add one tier at a time. Place the first tier and check to make sure it is level. I recommend that you use shims for the leveling process, preferably the plastic ones that you can buy at the lumber store. Place the shim until your lower tier is level. Make a mark on the shim, cut off the excess, and place it back under the tier. The remaining tiers should be already level if the base tier is level. Make sure you measure and level as you add each tier, as there may be a shift in the construction. You need to correct this error as it happens, not when it's all completed.

The pump fits nicely into the second-tier riser.

Installing the Pump

Installing your pump should be fairly straightforward. You probably have purchased a submersible pump that will be placed in the basin or lowest tier. Place the pump in the deeper part of the basin or lower tier so it draws water from the bottom of the basin. Connect the outlet of the pump to the tubing that brings the water to the top of the fountain. You'll want to hide the pump from view so place it at whatever is the "back" of the fountain. The cord will be a bit more difficult. You can use some silicone RTV to glue the cord in place and to help keep it from view.

Filling the Fountain

Use your garden hose and fill up the basin and each tier. If you forget to fill the tiers, the basin may become empty or low. Of course, you can just top up the basin, too. Depending on climate, you may have to top up your basin each day. Make sure that you keep an eye on the water level. If the water level falls too low, the pump may lose it's prime and seize. This is a common and costly mistake, as pumps are usually expensive.

Now you are ready to turn on your pump and adjust the flow until you get a water flow that you find pleasing. Then there is only one thing left to do. Sit back, relax, and enjoy your new fountain.

The finished fountain, filled and splashing.

Installing the Hidden Sump Fountain

Using a hidden sump is a great way to create a fountain for your garden without adding a visible pool, basin or pond. The method has become so popular that you can now find a sump kit in most garden shops.

Your choice for a fountain can be almost any object that catches your fancy. The only exception

Millstones work great as hidden sump fountains.

Here are the materials you will need to build a hidden sump fountain.

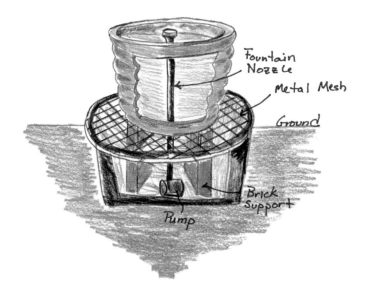

would be something that is a "spitter" or shoots the water a long distance away from the fountain.

The trick to a fountain with a hidden sump is that you bury the basin. The water from the fountain flows into the sump where the pump is positioned. The fountain will sit on a perforated cover over the sump. As always, the trick is to get the fountain level.

Fountain Ideas

Here are a few ideas for your hidden sump fountain. Almost anything will work, so you can be creative.

Overflowing Jar

There are so many nice ceramic and terra cotta jars and pots available for the water garden. Anyone could make a great overflowing jar fountain. Tip the jar on its side for a different look.

Ceramic jars also work well as hidden sump fountains.

Watering Can to Nowhere

This is very cute in a country style garden. Use a metal watering can tipped so that the water is flowing from the spout. You can use a metal pipe to elevate the can above your flowerbed so that it looks like the flowers are always being watered. The metal pipe can be used to hide the vinyl tubing by running the tubing inside the metal piping.

Umbrella Kids

A very popular statue is a child standing under an umbrella. Use some tubing to deliver water to the top of the umbrella and position the statue over the sump.

Installation

Things You will Need to Install a Hidden Sump Fountain:

1. Fountain

2. Pump and low-level cut off switch

3. Tubing matched in size to your pump outlet

4. Tubing clamp to adjust flow rate

5. Sump

6. Sump Cover

7. Electricity source to site (with GFIC of course)

8. Sand and finish rock

9. Cinder blocks and/or bricks (depends on sump cover)

10. Tools—shovel, level, razor knife, tubing cutter, small c-clamp, silicone RTV]

Bubbling Jar

Use the overflowing jar idea, but place a bubbler style fountain nozzle in the top of the jar.

Three-Tiered Fountain

Now you can let the water flow over the bottom tier into the sump. Make sure your sump or liner extends well beyond the diameter of the lowest tier, as the water has a tendency to splash a lot by the time it reached the bottom tier. This is especially true on windy days.

Your Pump

For a hidden sump fountain, the head required is the distance from the pump to the top of your fountain or jar where the water will be spilling over. I also strongly recommend that you purchase (and use) a float switch that will turn the pump off if the sump level falls too low.

The tubing is connected to the pump, and the unit is then lowered into the sump between the bricks.

Digging Required

After you have chosen your site, it is time to dig. Take your sump and trace an outline of it on the ground. Make the hole just a little larger than the sump and just as deep. Once you have finished digging the hole, test the fit by placing the sump in your new hole. After you feel satisfied by the fit, use a small shovel to make the bottom of the hole as level as possible.

The next step is to place a layer of sand on the bottom of the hole. You can use play sand or masonry sand for this. Compress the sand and level the sand as much as possible. The idea is to provide a level surface for the sump. If you have purchased a commercially made sump, follow the directions included. Again, test the fit and levelness of the sump in your hole until you are satisfied.

The hole is dug and made level using masonry sand.

Making Your Own Sump

You can use other containers as sumps to save money or if you cannot find a commercially made fountain sump. Plastic tubs, buckets, flowerpots, and garbage cans are all potential sumps. I recommend that you also use some sort of pond liner to wrap the sump with. This will help guard against excess water loss if there is a leak in the sump.

Using Pond Liners

You may wish to use a pond liner with a commercially made fountain sump. They make great splashguards and really help direct the water back into the sump. Pond liners are available in many grades and materials. You can use one of the better grades of rubber liner for your fountain project, but the less expensive vinyl will often work just as well. Buy a section of pond liner material that will extend one or two feet beyond your sump. When buying off a roll, just take the diameter or width of the sump and add four feet. This should be a sufficient rule of thumb for most standard-sized sumps.

Before you place your sump in the ground, place it open-side down on the liner and trace the outline of the sump onto the liner. Chalk or yellow tire marking pen will work best since your liner is black.

Bury Sump and Placing the Liner

There will be an open area between the edge of the hole and the sump. You can backfill this space with soil left over from your excavation or with the same type of sand you used to level the sump in the first place. Either way, you want this material to be well compacted into the space. I often use a small trickle of water from the garden hose to help compact it. Be careful though; if you use too much water you may lift up the sump and it will no longer level.

You can now place your liner. Trim the liner to the dimensions that you like and place the liner over the sump. Use a razor knife to make a small hole in the liner where it is centered over the sump. Then cut the liner toward the outer rim of the sump, stopping just short of the outer edge. You will end up with a series of triangular slices that fall into the sump from the liner. You can trim the ends off the triangles, or just leave them the way they are.

The sump has been placed and the dirt has been filled back in.

You want the liner to guide water back into the sump. I like to use silicone sealer to glue the liner flaps against the sides of the sump and seal anything that looks like a place for water to leak out of the sump. After the silicone has cured, you can use your hose to test the liner area. Wet down all of the liner and see if the water flows back into the sump. Some careful testing now can save you a lot of rework later.

Pump in the Sump

Now you are ready put your pump into the sump, and it is also the time to set up the low-level float switch. Affix the float to the side of the sump. A good way to do this is with a cheap C-clamp. Make sure you have adjusted the switch so that it shuts off the pump before the sump is completely empty.

The pump is in place, and it's time to feed the tubing up into the jar above.

I have assumed that you have prepared your electrical connection beforehand. Arrange the cords and plug the pump into the back of the plug for the level switch. The level switch *will not* work if you do not plug them in this way. Most level switches work this way, but check yours out ahead of time just in case as new styles are being developed all the time.

Attach your tubing to the outlet of your pump. Use a plastic hose clamp to firmly secure the tubing, so that you won't have to open things back up later if it should pop off. Metal clamps tend to rust apart after a season or two and usually fall off at the least of convenient times like during a party or family gathering. The hose clamps on your fountain pump should be the last concern you have to worry about when you are entertaining guests.

Cover Up

If you have made your own sump, you will need to find a good material to cover the sump. A piece of perforated steel is an excellent material but may be a little hard to find. If you are brave, call a few machine shops and look for scraps–you may find a real bargain. Expanded steel mesh is a similar material and will also work very well. Some other ideas for covers are replacement barbecue grills or rigid fencing materials.

The cover itself may not be strong enough to support your fountain or jar. Use cinder blocks and bricks to build a solid support that rises from the center of the sump to the top of the sump. This will give a firm support for your jar.

The tubing is threaded into the jar. Silicone sealant is then used to help prevent any leakage.

Before you lower the cover over the sump, feed the tubing through the mesh at a place close to where the fountain will stand. Don't place it where the fountain will sit on top of the tubing because the weight of the fountain can potentially pinch it closed. Now you can lower down your cover.

Stones

The best finish material for a hidden fountain sump is stone. You can find stones of different colors, shapes, and sizes. The only requirement is that the stone you choose should not be able to fall into the sump through the grate. If the same stone is used throughout the landscape, the sump will be much less obvious. You can also conceal the cords by using your landscaping stone.

Hidden Spittin'

The best way to set up a hidden spitting fountain is to use a second sump and connect the two with some extra plumbing. You will also need to place pond lining between the two sumps with a slight rise in the center of them, so that most stray drops will make it back to one sump or the other. Buy your fountain and pump before you start digging. You will need to test the pump and fountain combo to see where the stream of water will land so you know where to put the second sump. Remember that weather will have a serious role to play and you should take this into account.

Also, don't forget the low-level cut-off switch for the pump. On a windy day, you have the potential to lose water quickly, and you surely don't want to run the pump dry. Certainly, this is a more challenging design, but it could make a fun display in your garden.

Finishing

Using your garden hose, fill the sump up about three-quarters and turn on the pump. Your fountain will now fill from the water in the sump. Top up the sump as needed. If your fountain has a jar, you can fill up the jar too. Use the hose clamp to adjust the flow rate to suit your taste. The flow rate may take some time, be patient and check on it frequently over the first few days, so the correct adjustments can be made.

Installing a Wall Fountain

The history of wall fountains goes back to the Ancient Romans. Originally, they were built as a place to get water for the people's households, although some were meant for watering horses and other animals. The Romans built some magnificent aqueducts in order to supply water from remote regions to their cities.

Here is a great example of a lion's head wall fountain.

Multi-piece fountains such as this one are usually easy to install.

Whether your fountainhead is a lion or another symbol, the wall fountain adds a formal and classy look to any garden.

The lion's head fountain has become pervasive in almost every culture. The lion has represented nobility, pride, power, and strength since very ancient times. The lion's head was used as decoration all over the ancient world. Roman coins, door handles, and many more mundane objects were decorated with the head of a lion. Perhaps the water coming from the lion's mouth was meant to remind you that the Emperor's aqueduct delivered your water.

Where to Look

Wall fountains require a pool or basin below them since they are just "spitters" hung on a wall. Since fountains of all types have become so popular, you should have no problem finding a wall fountain that

Things You Will Need:

1. Fountain
2. Pump and low-level cut off switch
3. Tubing matched to pump outlet
4. Tubing clamp to adjust flow rate
5. Basin
6. Electricity source to site
7. Tools - level, tubing cutter, silicone RTV, masonry adhesive, drill, masonry screws]

you like. There is even a wide variety of indoor fountains available that offer various, and often unique, designs.

Many people use a wall-of-water effect in a more contemporary setting. In a wall-of-water design, there is a sheet of water that flows down the front of the fountain. High quality wall-of-water fountains are usually silent. That makes the especially favorable to those that would like a fountain indoors.

Water plants will do well in basins that receive an ample amount of sunlight.

Most of the commonly available wall fountains are made of lightweight materials that make hanging them much easier. The water itself is very heavy (the old pint's a pound rule) and heavy marble or other stone would certainly add to the weight.

Before or After?

It is much better to plan for a wall fountain before the wall is actually constructed. This will allow you to hide the tubing that connects the fountainhead to the pump in the basin. However, in most cases, the fountain will probably come after the wall. Of course, this will present some challenges as far as hiding the tubing is concerned. One way to avoid the problem is to purchase a wall fountain that has the basin and fountainhead as one unit. All you will have to do is hang the whole unit. These are rapidly becoming the most popular style, as they are perfect for small apartments and homes.

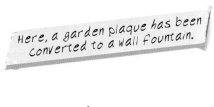

Here, a garden plaque has been converted to a wall fountain.

Attach Your Head

The first step is to attach the fountainhead to the wall; some may already have predrilled holes for attachments. You can use masonry screws to attach the fountain to the wall. You will need a good electric drill for this and the correct type and size of screws. If you have doubts, you can ask for assistance at your local hardware retailer.

Another good option is to use glue formulated for outdoors. Look for something that says it will work on masonry and is for outdoor use. Put the glue on all of the surfaces that will stick to the wall. *Don't forget* to attach the tubing to the fountainhead before you glue it onto the wall. I recommend that you attach an extra-long length of tubing to the fountainhead because you can easily trim it to the correct length if it turns out being too long. On the other hand, it would be a unfortunate to find out that your tubing is too short to make it to the pump after you have glued it to the wall.

Tubing Trouble

If you cannot hide the tubing behind the wall, you have to be creative with ways to hide it. Here are a few ideas.

• Glue it to the wall.

• Paint the tubing to match the wall.

• Place a climbing plant in a pot next to the basin let the plant climb the tubing.

Part 1

• Put a trellis on the wall below the fountainhead and the basin. Again, hide the tubing with a climbing plant.

The Basin

Measure both the fountainhead and the basin, finding the center points of each. You should line up the center of the fountainhead– usually the hole where the water comes out–to the center of the basin and line them up with each other.

This is a good example of a common, three-tiered wall fountain.

You will need to make certain that your basin is level. The "excavate and sand" method can be used if the basin sits on the ground. If the basin is placed on a solid surface, especially indoors, then use a few shims to level the basin. Test the level before you make the final attachment to the wall.

When you have everything set up for final placement, put some of your glue on the back of your basin. Fit everything into place and level before the glue dries. It usually takes most adhesives sometime before they completely set, so you probably won't have to rush but check the suggested drying time on the label to be certain.

Finally, seal around the basin with a grout or bathtub sealer. It would be fine to skip this step, but caulking gives a more finished look.

Finishing Up

All that is left is to attach the pump, fill up your new fountain, and plug it in. You can also consider installing a low-level cut-off switch for your pump. This is an especially good idea if you are not home all the time to check the water level. It is never good for pumps to run dry for a long period of time, as this may cause the pump's impeller to overheat and seize in the impeller housing.

Caring for Your Pond-Based Fountain

The fountains of ancient times required very little care for one reason–they had an endless supply of clean water flowing in and out of them. You probably will not be so lucky. Your fountain will be re-circulating the same water over and over again, so it is very important to understand how to properly maintain it. Smelly or green

Plants, such as these water lilies, help keep pond water clear by blocking out sun.

water spraying out of your fountain is not very appealing, so let's go over the best ways to keep your new fountain sparkling and fresh.

Pond-Based Fountains

If your fountain is a part of a larger pond, the quality of the pond water will be your main concern. Let's take a look at the problems you may encounter with your pond and fountain water.

Green Goopy Water

Green water is the most common problem in ponds. It is especially common in the spring. Algae would be the cause in this instance. There are many types of algae, such as hair or filamentous, slime, encrusting, and free-floating algae. The alga responsible for making your pond appear as if it is filled up with green pea soup is the free-floating algae.

This water garden shows a variety of water plants that you can choose from.

Because algae are photosynthetic like plants, everything you know about plants goes for algae. They need sunlight and nutrients to grow and thrive. Your strategy for dealing with a bloom should include cutting it off from the things it needs.

You can cut down on the sunlight that reaches the algae in your pond by adding more floating plants that help shade the surface of the water. Lily pads will cover the surface of the water pretty well, but water hyacinths and water lettuces float on the surface and block out much more light. If you're fighting an algae bloom, you should try to cover about 50 percent of the open water. Depending on the climate in which you live, your pond should be 60 to 75 percent covered with floating plants by the middle of summer.

Plants are also in direct competition against algae for the nutrients in your pond. A water garden that is heavily stocked with a balanced variety of plants should consume most of the nutrients, therefore preventing a large algae bloom. This is one reason why natural ecosystems remain well balanced and suffer only occasional algae blooms.

Changing some of the water in your pond on a regular basis will make a big difference. Algae blooms are very common in the spring because the other plants in your water garden have not yet completely come back to life, but water changes can dilute the nutrients that sustain algae. Most of these spring blooms will simply pass with time and only require a little shade and a partial water change.

Chemicals that Fight Algae

You will see several types of algaecides, which are products available to help reduce and kill algae blooms. The problem with algaecides is that, if used in high doses, they can kill the good things

Clear pond water means clear fountain spray. The last thing you want is for your fountain to look as if it's spraying pea soup.

in ponds like your plants. They usually provide only temporary relief, because the conditions that caused the algae bloom may still be present after the effects of the algaecides are long gone. However, the algaecides normally give you some time to figure out a better solution. If your fountain is part of your pond, use these chemicals as a last resort.

Another class of products that helps remove algae is called flocculants. They work by getting the algae to stick together in large blobs that sink to the bottom of the pond. I have tried these products and they do work temporarily. However, they don't kill the algae, and your pump might just break up the clumps all over again, so you definitely need a good solids-removal filter to make headway with flocculants.

Finally, there are products available that are essentially dark-blue dyes. The idea is that the dye will absorb all the light the algae would need to grow. Dyes will work but may appear very unsightly, and most people will cringe when they see them. Your water garden will look like it has a toilet treatment in it rather than appearing natural. Natural water is not dark blue–at least not the fake blue of these dyes.

Using Ultraviolet Light

If you have a full-blown bloom, a UV clarifier will probably take care of it in a few days. The UV light can also prevent a bloom from getting going in the first place by killing the algae as soon as it divides. I personally like UV as a solution when shade or water changes fail. Another benefit is

A shallow stream leading to a pond is a great natural filter of excessive nutrients.

that it will kill protozoa and bacteria that may affect your fish or plants. UV is in discriminatory, however, and should only be used on systems that have been cycled for at least a few months.

In the spring, you will want to run your UV clarifier constantly to prevent an initial algae bloom. I found that I could turn mine off once the plants were lush and full with no further algae outbreaks and the fish all appear to be normal and active. It also allows me to save a little electricity, too.

Part 1

The Dead Bodies

An algae bloom itself does not harm your fish or plants. The only potential problem is at night, when photosynthesis is reversed and the algae begin to use up oxygen and release carbon dioxide. If you have a lot of algae, your fish could end up suffocating at night. The problem is compounded in the summer, when the water holds less oxygen anyway because the water is warmer—water is not capable of holding high levels of oxygen at higher temperatures. Make sure you have plenty of aeration in your pond, especially when there is an algae bloom. Running your fountain through the night is a great way to help your pond if you do have an algae bloom.

As the bloom dies off, there will be a lot of waste in your pond as the dead algae piles up. Water changes will help remove this, but you may also have to wash you particle filter more frequently until the solids are removed. Make an effort to keep up with the waste as the bloom ends, so that you do not have further problems with the water quality.

If you have a basin, jar, or other type of fountain that can hold some water plants, adding some will naturally keep your water clean.

Odor Problems

If you sense a rotten, swampy, egg smell, you could have an anaerobic spot (a spot without oxygen) in the pond or filter. If oxygen does not get to the water because the circulation has stopped, or if you have a dead spot (a spot without circulation), such as the bottom of a thick pile of detritus, anaerobic bacteria multiply there. These anaerobic bacteria use sulfur as an energy source instead of oxygen, which is why they give off hydrogen sulfide gas. The situation requires immediate action.

If this has happened in your pond, then you need to do a large water change right away. The buildup of hydrogen sulfide gas can quickly kill all your fish.

In large fountains, you may need the assistance of chemicals to keep the water clear.

Open your bottom drain to release at least 20 percent of the water. Drain and wash down your filters. Keep an eye on the behavior of your fish. If they seem to be gasping for air, spending a lot of time at the surface, or if the water still smells, do another water change in a day or two.

The best prevention is to keep up with your pond maintenance and not let the detritus build up in the bottom of the pond or in the filters. You don't need to find the anaerobic spot, but you do need to keep the water well oxygenated (and the pond clean) to prevent the anaerobic bacteria from finding a home.

Plants

Oxygenating plants live their lives submerged in the water. In strong light, they liberate oxygen directly into the water, as often observed by tiny bubbles formed on their leaves. They can also act as natural water softeners by reducing the mineral content of the water and will compete with free-floating algae for nutrients to help reduce or eliminate an algae bloom. You can buy oxygenating plants in bunches and place them in your basin or jar or anywhere they can receive direct sunlight. Use a lead plant-tie to help sink them to the bottom.

Your best choices of submerged pond plants are the species *Anacharis* and hornwort. Anacharis (*Egeria densa*) is the most common submerged plant that you will find. Anacharis has small green leaves that are compactly whorled around a brittle stem. The stem can break easily, but a new plant will grow. In very warm water, above 75°F, the plants may become lanky. Hornwort (*Ceratophyllum demersum*) may even produce algae-suppressing chemicals into the water and it will grow very rapidly. In the fall, the compact tips break off the plant and fall to the bottom of the container.

Cloudy, green-colored water is not appealing.

Water Changes and Chemicals

When your fountain water gets icky, just change it, because you shouldn't have any fish in there that could be potentially shocked by such a drastic water change. Pump it all out and replace it with new water. In the summer, you may need to do this more often. If this is incon-

The draining and refilling of your fountain is sometimes needed

venient or expensive (watch your water bill), try using chemicals to extend the life between water changes. There are various types and grades of chemical filtration on the market that will help you in prolonging the life of your fountain water. Look for something that will not be toxic to any birds or animals that may come to drink from your fountain.

Part Two
Wonderful Waterfalls

"Having a garden waterfall is great, but I wish the squirrels would stop going down in little barrels."

Introduction to
Waterfalls

Moving water adds so much to your garden pond, both aesthetically and biologically. The sound of water running over a waterfall or through a stream is extremely soothing and is a proven stress reliever. The sound and the motion will add a new dimension to your garden. The waterfall and pool may also become a refuge for various species wildlife around your house. Many species of wild birds will drink

Gentle side fall at Anna Ruby Falls, Georgia.

These rocks are an integral part of Dukes Falls, Georgia.

and bathe in the waterfall on a regular basis. Small animals, like mice and voles, may also use it as a place to drink. Frogs and toads will mysteriously arrive to make your pool a focus for their spring mating. Even some species of small (and not-so-small) snakes may show up to take a drink, too. You will see animals that you probably didn't know were your neighbors.

Waterfalls hold a special interest for people as well. National parks, hiking trails, and many tourist spots feature waterfalls. Think of all the honeymooners that have gone to Niagara Falls. I have hiked four miles on the Na Pali coast of Kauai in Hawaii just to look at a special waterfall there. The cold spray and spectacular sight were rewards for all my hard work in getting there, and swimming in the cold pool at the base of the fall was a special thrill.

Garden Ponds and Waterfalls

There are practical reasons to adding a waterfall to an existing water garden. Waterfalls and streams help add oxygen to the water for your fish. You will probably have a pump that pulls water out of your pond and through your filter, so why not get the water back into the pond in a more interesting way than just a return nozzle? If you did not build a waterfall at the start of your pond project, don't worry–it really isn't a problem to add one at a later date.

You are going to be looking for a place to hide your pond filter system, and behind or inside a waterfall is a great place to put this.

The bigger the flow, the bigger the show at Anna Ruby Falls, Georgia.

You could build a filter house, and construct your waterfall around it with a door in the back to access the filter. This would be well hidden behind the waterfall but would still allow easy access.

A waterfall does not have to be really high to be pleasing, but if you have a good site that allows some height, use it. It is best to have your waterfall drop into a small pool before entering your pond and then spill over into the main pond as to avoid agitating the water in the main pond too much.

You can establish several levels in the waterfall as to make your waterfall more interesting. If you make each level a little wider, you will create an effect that makes your waterfall appear to be larger. You will also decrease the velocity of the water on each level, so that its final drop into the pond is not overly vigorous.

Waterfall to Nowhere

Remember the fountain to nowhere? You can use a similar technique to build your waterfall. The reservoir at the end of the fall may need to be larger (depending on your fall), but all in all, it is still a manageable design. Just use the grate over the reservoir and let the fall end there. You should carefully consider placement so that the result is not too unnatural. I prefer to have a pool at the end of the fall to better mimic a natural setting.

Here, water is flowing from two different directions, creating an interesting effect.

Streams and Water Courses

If you think about it, a stream is just a waterfall that doesn't fall. They are sloped so the water will flow to one end, but there is no major falls built into it. A stream added to a garden pond offers the same benefits as a waterfall. You are also providing a large natural filter for your pond by having the water flow over a long bed of various sized rocks as the rocks will help to mechanically help remove suspended particles.

A watercourse is really just a stream–what makes them differ is the design. For a stream you try to emulate nature. A watercourse can use a variety of designs.

It's small, but all of the elements of a waterfall are there.

Most of these designs are contrived or man-made looking and can come in a wide variety of styles that lead the water in different directions or around small islands, and eventually into a pool at the end. The water is then returned to the beginning by a pump. Pumps for watercourses and streams have to be very powerful due to the far distances the water has to travel.

9

Planning your Waterfall

With a little effort, you can enjoy the sights and sounds of a waterfall right in your own backyard. If you have a hill in your yard, this would be the best place to put your own fall. The higher the fall, the more energy the water will have, which means a more satisfying fall. Remember that water splashing into a pond from a heightened level can be noisy, so you may

Use perspective to make the waterfall appear larger than it really is.

Part 2

want to incorporate a timer on your waterfall's pump system, so you don't keep the neighbors awake at night.

If you do not have a hill, don't worry. You can build one. Many people use the soil that was removed when digging their pond to build a waterfall. What a great use of your extra dirt. If necessary, you can also buy dirt, usually very inexpensively, to create your waterfall.

Pumps

Waterfalls are all about gravity. Falling water creates a great show of sight and sound. But how high should you build your waterfall? You must include the height of your waterfall in your pump calculation. This part is easy: Just add a foot of head loss for each foot high that you pump the water. However, the higher you go, the harder it may be to find a pump to handle the job.

I recently looked at the pump curves for some of the more commonly used pond pumps, and I found that in most cases there is

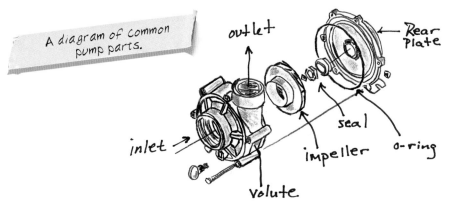

A diagram of common pump parts.

a foot or two of head to spare. This means you can build a waterfall a foot or two higher than your calculations prove without having to get a more powerful pump. If you already have a pond, check with the pump manufacturer for the specifications on your pump to see if you can run your filter and waterfall from the same pump.

If you want a really large and magnificent waterfall, your water pump may not be able to supply enough flow. In this case, buy a separate pump for the waterfall or stream. You would size this pump exactly the same way you would for a fountain (see the Making Preparations chapter). Select your desired flow rate and the head required for your waterfall. Remember that if you wing it and just pick a pump based on flow rate, you may end up with a pump that will cost too much money to run, or it may not even pump the water up to the top of the waterfall.

Know The Flow

A rule of thumb for deciding how much flow you want for your waterfall is to use from 50 to 100 gallons per hour for every one inch of waterfall. A flow rate in this range will give a lip of water that is up to a half-inch high. Therefore, if you want your waterfall to be eight inches wide, you will want a flow of 400 to 800 gallons per hour for your pump.

The half-inch high refers to the height of the water right at the top of the waterfall before it drops over the edge. That does not mean the water falls half an inch. In fact, once you pump the water over

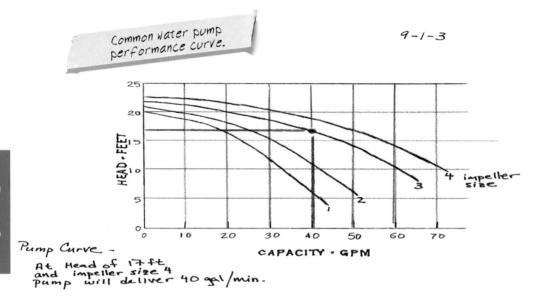

Common water pump performance curve.

9-1-3

Pump Curve -
At Head of 17 ft
and impeller size 4
Pump will deliver 40 gal/min.

the edge of the waterfall, it does not take any extra energy to make it fall–gravity does that for you. So your water can fall as much as you like. The half-inch buildup at the lip of the falls gives it enough energy to fall away from the edge and not just dribble over.

You could use less than 100 gallons per inch of width, but then the height of the water at the very lip of the fall will be less than half an inch. The less the flow, the more like a trickle the waterfall will be.

Next you need to estimate the head loss to the waterfall, which is the height from the pump to the waterfall and a little more for the tubing. Add half a foot for the tubing. If the tubing is very long or has lots of bends, you may need to do a more involved calculation.

This recommendation gives you a pleasing amount of water coming over the fall. It's hard to define "pleasing," but the idea is that you want a vigorous enough flow for it to seem like a good waterfall–not just a little trickle.

The more water that flows over a waterfall, the farther the water will project out over the edge of the waterfall. You may have to play around with your flow rate to get the most pleasing effect. If it's projecting out too far, you can always put a T-junction in the plumbing and direct part of the flow back to the pond. You will be able to adjust the flow to your liking this way.

Part 2

Rocks Are Best

Waterfalls need rocks. If you have rocks in your yard, here is a good place to use them. However, you will probably have to buy rocks for your project. When you buy rocks for the pond itself, look for a few interesting ones for your waterfall or stream.

Big rocks for big waterfalls. Wakoola Water gardens.

When selecting that special stone for the lip of the waterfall, think about what you would like the falls to look like. A flat stone will create a solid sheet of water

A good imitation of a super-slow-flow water-fall. Not all falls need to be rapids.

falling over the edge. If you use many boulders, you will have a rapids effect. Also have some small stones and gravel on hand to fill in the entire waterfall; small stones and gravel are great filler in a waterway.

When you select any rocks for your pond, be sure to select ones that have a low limestone content. Granite, slate, and shale are all interesting choices, and don't have much limestone. When in doubt, do the soak test. Soak your rock in a bucket for a few days and test the pH of the water. If it measures over 8.0 on the pH scale, you probably shouldn't use that rock. Be sure to measure the starting pH for reference. That way, you'll know the pH value of your tap water and can then compare the two values to each other.

Plumbing for Waterfalls

A lot of effort can go into building a waterfall. If it is a large one, it will require even more effort. I am sure you have done the calculations you need to make sure that the pump will be sending enough water to the fall, but what about the plumbing?

Every inch of pipe you need adds to the head loss in the total system. Remember that smaller diameter pipe has higher head losses. The first thing you need to do is choose the correct diameter piping. If the waterfall is a large one, pay for larger piping, as this will make your life easier later on.

Think carefully about where you put the plumbing. My preference is to place it where you can get to it later without taking the whole waterfall apart. Definitely bury it to get it out of sight, but you'll have to decide how much work you are willing to do to dig the piping up later.

Plants transform ordinary water gardens into gorgeous displays.

Tubing for Small Waterfalls

Small waterfalls can use a submerged pump and tubing to deliver the water to the top of the waterfall. I recommend that you use a small plastic pan to make a small pool at the top of the waterfall. If the water just sprayed out of the pipe, the flow down the rocks would be less satisfying than when the pan is used. The pan has a nice lip to spread the water out and make a nice flow down the rocks. You may be able to purchase a pan like this or build one yourself.

You can place the tubing for smaller waterfalls underneath the rocks, preferably to the side of the waterfall. The tubing should be covered with the same rocks used to make the waterfall. In this case, all you have to do is move a few rocks to get to the piping, and the tubing is concealed from view.

Large Diameter Tubing for Large Waterfalls

A larger waterfall will require a larger pump and therefore larger diameter tubing. The larger the diameter of the tubing, the easier it is to kink. Look for kink-free tubing from a pond supply store. You should be able to find it up to a two-inch diameter. The larger the installation, the more care you should take when installing your plumbing. You would not want to disassemble your waterfall due to poor construction from a rushed job. Place the tubing in a location where you can get to it if needed and make sure you take your time. Measure twice then cut.

Using slate to cover the actual fall is a great way to help hide the origins of the water.

You should use a T-connection for large waterfalls, giving you more control over the flow rate. Use the T to divert water back to the main pond. If you split the stream, how can you make sure you get the amount of water you want going to the waterfall? Think about the head loss in pipes again. If the pipes were the same size, as in this figure, you will probably get more flow going right back to the pond than going to the waterfall. You can customize this design very easily by adding a valve to the outlet of the pipe where it goes back to the pond. Closing the valve will send more water to the fall.

Using Utilities

Please review the safety information in the Making Preparations chapter. Everything mentioned about electricity dangers for fountains apply to ponds and waterfalls too. Keep the installation of your waterfall as safe as possible.

Depending on the type of pump you are using, you will want to have power close to your site. I think it is worth the money to have an electrician install a power line and outlet to the location. You can tackle this yourself if you feel comfortable, but why not get someone who has experience utilizing electricity? Do not forget where your line runs so that you do not cut into it doing other work around the site. It is best to install electricity after work with heavy machinery is completed.

Installing a Liner-Based Waterfall

Using liner materials as the base for a waterfall is probably the most popular method. You will have many choices for liner material, but EPDM rubber is by far the most resilient and long lasting material. Even if your pond liner is not EPDM, you should consider investing in EPDM for the waterfall liner. The liner is the base material for your

A common-type of liner-based pond and waterfall.

waterfall so if it leaks, you will have to dismantle the entire waterfall.

A liner-based waterfall should be considered a nearly permanent addition to your yard. The good-quality liner can last over 20 years, and, of course, the rocks are not going anywhere.

Design Details and Hardware

It is important to plan out all of the elements of your waterfall design and gather as many materials as you can before you begin–going backward during the construction will certainly be very frustrating. Let's discuss the hardware that you will need for your waterfall and how they will impact your design.

These plastic containers would make good intermediate basins for a waterfall.

First, you will be able to find all of these waterfall parts available commercially. Ten years ago, I would have been telling you how to improvise many of these parts using common items. The downside to this is that, as the availability of parts went up, so did some of the costs. In many cases, using the best parts is well worth the expense, but sometimes there are alternatives that will save you money. The following are some of these alternatives.

Money-saving Hardware Alternatives

Pumps

This is your most important piece of waterfall hardware and probably the most expensive item on your list. Make sure your pump will provide the flow rate you need to the desired height (head). Pump selection will also affect the cost in operating your waterfall because some pumps are more energy efficient than others. Many can make your electricity bill go through the roof. *Do not* use a sump pump meant for pumping out a basement! They won't last long enough and they use too much electricity.

Tubing

The best material available is kink-free tubing that is still flexible. The larger the tubing diameter, the more expensive it is however. You can also use rigid PVC pipe that can be purchased at home improvement stores. You will need to "hard" pipe bends by using different fittings. This will lead to more head loss than tubing, but rigid PVC pipe is much less expensive.

Basins

I like to incorporate a basin at the top and bottom of a waterfall. The basin at the top will help the flow pattern of your waterfall by making it easy to create a level lip for the water to fall from. Many pond kits now include a waterfall basin that also acts as the biological filter for your pond. Great idea but can be a pricey item. If you are a confident, do-it-yourself individual, try using a large plastic tub or plastic garbage can instead. You will need to create your own lip, and it must be level and flat.

I also like to add a fairly long bottom basin, especially if the waterfall has a lower flow rate. A lot of gravel and small rocks do the job of garbage collecting. It is always a good thing to keep the debris out of your pond.

Drains

The biggest mistake that pond builders make, in my opinion, is to leave out drains. You will find it so much easier to clean up your pond if you can just drain out the detritus. That means you need a drain wherever detritus will collect. The bottom of the pond, filters, and basins are all good places to have drains. It is also best have a drain with a good-sized opening, at least an inch and a half. To clean up, open your drains and the detritus will flow away. This is a great thing when you want to perform a water change while removing excessive detritus buildup.

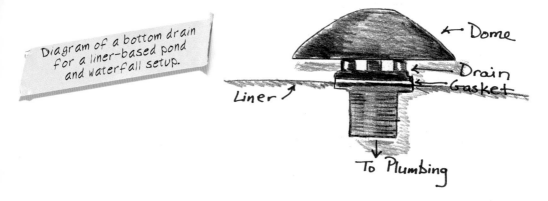

Diagram of a bottom drain for a liner–based pond and waterfall setup.

Liners

You definitely want to purchase your liner before you begin digging. The problem with buying liner for a waterfall project is that you may have to buy more liner material than you will need for the project due to the width of the liner roll. You can piece together smaller pieces of liner to be more economical. This just depends on your personal preference and budget. I think using several pieces of liner is fine as long as you use them carefully.

This is the author's liner-based waterfall. Wakoola Watergardens.

Design Ideas

Your landscape will probably dictate the slope of your waterfall. If you have a slight slope the waterfall may be more like a stream and that is perfectly fine. If you can use a steeper hill, your waterfall will usually be much more dramatic. You can build up the slope for your waterfall, but be careful or you may end up with something that looks like a termite mound sticking up out of your ground. The most natural looking waterfall will result from using your existing land contours.

You can also use the trick of perspective to make your waterfall seem larger. If you have ever done any painting or drawing, you have probably learned of this technique to give objects a sense of three-dimensional appearance. Simply put, you will build the top of the waterfall narrower than the bottom.

To have the technique work most effectively, you will need to have an even transition from the top to the bottom. If you drew this design on paper, you would draw a line that angles from the top to the bottom. With your waterfall, you do exactly the same, just use some string as your "perspective guide". You can enhance you illusion by matching the size of the stones to their position on the waterfall. Use the larger stones at the bottom, small stones on top.

Preparing Your Site

The first step in building your waterfall is the site excavation. The first thing you should do is set up your "perspective lines" if you are using this method. Remove the top layer of grass and soil. You can cut into your hill to create "steps" and "basins" as you descend the hill. If your hill is long you can even consider taking a turn on the way down to make the fall look even longer.

If you decide to use a waterfall type filter, you can use some of your excavated soil to cover the filter. You also have the option to partially bury the waterfall top basin or filter vessel. If the top lip of the waterfall rises slightly above the level of the top of the hill you will reduce the amount of rainwater that will flow down the waterfall. Rainwater can drag soil and lawn chemicals into your pond so you need to take necessary precautions.

Remove all excess soil from your site and sharpen up any edges of you fall to suit your design. You can also dig in any depressions for intermediate basins at this time. You will now be ready to lay down your liner. Using a shovel will give you the best control during your excavation.

Suffering a heavy rainfall before you have put the liner down can erode your design and potentially drag a lot of mud into your pond. If you are using a basin at the bottom of the waterfall, you can install it temporarily to catch any mud. Another option is to cover the area where the waterfall is being constructed and hang a tarp over it. You can tilt the tarp in the direction you wish the water to go so as to prevent any soil or other unwanted materials to be washed into it. However, take these precautions only if you think you will have to

If your waterfall is being constructed in an area with a lot of soil then you will want to cover it when it starts to rain.

Part 2

take time between the excavation and the liner placement.

Top Basin and Plumbing

Your next step is to place the top basin. First, get your plumbing installed into the basin. You will have tubing or pipe that will connect the basin to your pump and possible a drain for the basin. You can also place your tubing down the side of the hill at this time. You can bury it or place it where you will be covering it with rocks and landscaping materials. Don't put the tubing under the waterfall itself. You may want to be able to have access to it later if necessary.

I recommend a T in the line to your waterfall. This gives you flexibility to adjust the flow rate to the waterfall, or even turn the waterfall completely off while running the pump.

Top basin in action. Wakoola Water gardens.

Installing your Liner

Placing your liner should not be too difficult. You will simply drape your excavation with the liner and carefully push the liner into place over any built-in steps and basins. Carefully work the liner into corners and contours. Don't worry about small folds in the liner where you must crease it to get a fit. You will be covering all of it with rocks later.

You can work top to bottom if you only have one piece of liner material. However, if you are using multiple pieces of liner you must work from the bottom to the top. Place the pieces of liner so that the piece that is higher on the hill laps over the top of the liner below it. Make sure that the bottom-most piece laps into your pond or pool. It is also a good idea to run a bead of silicone sealer under the flaps where they join.

Rocks that are placed artfully in and around the waterfall completely hide the liner.

On the outer edge of your waterfall, create a lip of soil to contain and guide the water. You want the liner to extend beyond the watercourse six inches to a foot. Think about water and how it flows. You want it to stay inside the waterfall. Finding leaks later can ruin your whole day.

Rock It!

Next task is the most interesting and possibly the hardest part of the job, rock placement. Your best artistic skills will be needed to place your waterfall stones to create a natural and realistic arrangement. Use a variety of sizes in different positions to make the arrangement

Rocks are placed around the pond and waterfall. Wakoola Water gardens.

look more random. Place your stones carefully and look at each one as you place it. If it doesn't seem right in a certain place - move it.

If you do a good job placing your stones, you may not need to use mortar or sealer to join the stones together. There is no problem if you decide to use mortar, just remember that it will take a little while to cure and will temporarily raise the pH of your pond. There are also commercially available polymeric foams that you can use instead of mortar.

I like to use a flat stone to attach to the lip for the top of the waterfall. This gives a smooth platform to launch the water to the waterfall. To get flow over the whole rock, use a level. You can use a bead of silicone sealer to keep the water from flowing off the sides of the rock.

After you have placed the large stones use gravel to fill in between rocks and cover places where the liner is showing. The gravel looks more natural than bare liner and will provide surface area for biological filtration.

Wet Test

When you have everything put together and you feel that it is all perfect, start up your pump. If you have been careful, everything should work just fine. You will probably have to add water to your pond as the basins of your waterfall fill up. If you notice that the level of your pond falls, you may have a leak. Look for wet places in the surrounding landscape—-a liner leak may show up nearby. It is also possible that the waterfall itself is splashing too much water out of the fall. You can adjust your rocks while the pump is running to fix any places where the water is splashing out. You will loose some water to evaporation but you probably will not see your pond level drop over a 24-hour period simply due to evaporation.

Part 2

Excellent Aquariums start with TROPICAL FISH HOBBYIST

SAVE UP TO **63%**

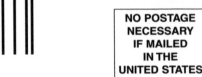

NO POSTAGE
NECESSARY
IF MAILED
IN THE
UNITED STATES

BUSINESS REPLY MAIL
FIRST-CLASS MAIL   PERMIT NO. 65   NEPTUNE, NJ

TROPICAL FISH HOBBYIST
SUBSCRIPTION DIVISION
P.O. Box 427
Neptune, NJ 07754-9989

Installing a Preformed Plastic Waterfall

There are basically two types of preformed plastic waterfalls. The first type of unit is a self-contained waterfall or water-course, while the second type uses a series of more plain basins to create a waterfall. I think both methods need a certain level of creativity, and preformed waterfalls should be limited to small-scale projects.

Artful landscaping hides the hill that was built to raise this waterfall.

Fortunately, the amount of work required to install preformed units will be much less than with a liner-based fall. There will be much less digging and much less rock lifting. However, only use this method for a small space, a flowerbed, or a tucked-away corner. You will be disappointed if you expect a large centerpiece using a preformed unit.

Preformed Waterfalls

A preformed waterfall is a good companion to a preformed pond, and they are commonly found at home improvement stores. Look for one that does not have a fake rock texture because these tend to look weathered after some time. The preformed pond and waterfall will have an edge that looks very finished. My preference is to use this type of pond in a flowerbed and arrange plants around the perimeter of the pond. A raised bed is an especially good home for this type of pond.

Preformed water-falls are often easily added on to larger ponds in the future.

The most important part of the installation of any preformed pond unit is leveling. You will excavate a hole for the pond and use elevation for the waterfall unit. Take your pond or waterfall unit and trace an outline of it on the ground. Now you need to start digging. Make the hole just a little larger in diameter than the preformed unit, but keep the depth the same as the preformed unit. Once you have finished digging the hole, test the fit by placing the preformed pond in your new hole. After you feel satisfied by the fit, use a small shovel to make the bottom of the hole as level as possible.

Not all preformed waterfall basins are small. Preformed ponds can also be used for larger projects.

The next step is to place a layer of sand on the bottom of the hole. You can use play sand or masonry sand. Compress and level the sand so you can provide a level surface for the pond/waterfall unit. Again, test the fit and levelness of the unit in your hole until you are satisfied that it is level. You can then backfill around the pond and waterfall with soil, making sure to pack the soil firmly around the preformed unit.

A preformed waterfall will have a predetermined angle for the fall. You can excavate your hill to accommodate the preformed unit. If you need to build a hill, the work will be similar. Because preformed

Part 2

units are pretty small, a tiny hill sticking up may look. Use your best judgment when making your incline.

Plumbing Your Preformed Waterfall

In every project, you want to make your plumbing as invisible as possible. If you are installing a pond and waterfall, investing in a small filter system is wise. You can find pump and filter combinations that are totally submersible. These are good choices as long as you don't mind putting your hand down in the pond when it is time to clean the filter.

Handy little units, such as this one, can be moved around your yard or garden.

Look into using bulkhead fittings for preformed units. The fitting is designed to screw around the hole and seal it as well. They are sometimes expensive, but they are the best fitting for the job and worth the money. Most will have pipe thread fittings, and because they are female on one side and male on the other, you will need some other adapters to hook up to the bulkhead fitting. A barbed to thread fitting will be your best bet. You can order online or look in your local plumbing supply outlet.

If you go to a home improve-ment store, look in several departments for your fittings. Plumbing, sprinkler systems, and water treatment systems will all have different types of fittings. You may need to hunt around to find exactly what you need. Don't forget hose clamps on the outside of those hose barbs because, if a hose gets loose, you can pump your pond down to nothing.

The waterfall of dreams.

Part 2

Finishing Up

I think that this is the hardest part of using a preformed pond or waterfall. I do like the neat edge, but giving it a ring of rocks just doesn't cut it for me. Rocks are fine, but they need to be blended into the landscaping. Using gravel and more rocks will help. Grass and other natural plantings near the pond will also help give a more natural look. Use your imagination for finishing your small pond and waterfall. It will be your creation–enjoy the process of getting there, as well as the finished product.

Building a Stream

The main difference between a stream and a waterfall is that a stream simply is not as high. Many of the steps for building a stream are similar to those used in constructing waterfalls, but I will point out how streams differ.

You can also build a stream with other methods, including poured concrete and preformed units.

The high flow of this natural stream creates white water.

Because using a liner is probably the best method, we will just talk about liner-based streams.

Design Details and Hardware

The materials that you will need are exactly the same as a liner waterfall; only the design will be slightly different. There can actually be a fine line between what is a waterfall and what would be called a stream. You could have a "stream" that takes its time wandering down a big hill. Your stream can take a few turns and even have a basin or two along the way for water plants. Just keep a gentle decline along the way to promote the flow of the water. Use your imagination to blend your stream into your landscape. Also, don't forget to use the perspective trick. Make the stream a little wider as you get closer to the pond to make it appear longer.

A large rock situated in a natural stream draws the eye.

The other important point is that water still runs downhill. There is no way you can get a stream to run uphill; it won't work, so don't try it. You can, however, build a stream on fairly level ground. You will need to excavate the area for the stream so that it gently gets deeper the closer you get to your pond or pump. There is no reason that you cannot use a hidden sump as the end point for your stream. A pond is the more traditional end for a stream and will probably work out better for you and your pond.

Stream Pitfalls

The amount of water contained in your stream can become a huge pitfall. Your pond or sump will be full of water–let's say 100 gallons. Your stream will also be full of water–about another 75 gallons (it's a really long stream). So, because a stream runs downhill, what will happen when your pump is turned off? You will soon have 175 gallons of water in your 100-gallon pond, and your pond will overflow. A well-designed pond should have some way to accommodate overflow. You can design a way for the water to run off or, even better, install an overflow pipe to direct the excess water away from the pond.

The second problem arises when you shut off your pump and want to start it back up again. Let's take the same pond, which has 100 gallons

In nature, streams often wind through the landscape.

Part 2

in the pond and 75 gallons in the stream. When you shut off your pump, the 75 gallons of water in the stream drain away through your overflow pipe. Now you want to start up again. At this point, there's 100 gallons in the pond. However, after you turn on the pump, eventually there will be only 25 gallons left in the pond, because the water from the pond is needed to replenish the water missing from the stream. This is a bad situation for your fish and water plants. You will need to stand by and refill your pond as the pump runs until you get a total of 175 gallons in the entire pond and stream again.

You can see that if your pump happens to shut off and then come back on while you aren't home, you can come home to a problem. One solution is to build a bigger pond so that the volume of water in the stream is not more than 10 or 20 percent of the total. Another potential solution is to have an automatic filling valve set up on your pond. If the level gets too low, the water will come on.

Pumps

The pump you need for a stream will require you to follow the same design rules that were used for waterfalls. You need to know the desired flow rate and the head (height) for the fall. Use the same rule of thumb for your stream; 50 to 100 gallons per hour per inch of stream (the width of your stream.) The head loss will be much different, however. The height will usually be much less than a waterfall. The head loss due to the length of tubing will go up. If your tubing run is very long, you may need to calculate this loss.

Tubing

The best material available is kink-free tubing that is also flexible. The larger the tubing diameter, the more expensive it is, however. You can also use rigid PVC pipe that can be purchased at home improvement stores. You will need to "hard" pipe bends by using different fittings. This will lead to more head loss than tubing, but rigid PVC pipe is much less expensive. You may need to calculate the head loss due to the tubing for a very long stream. The loss will be greatest for small diameter tubing and for many fittings, bends, or corners.

Basins

Basins are a very nice addition to a stream. You can use a variety of preformed basins or small ponds, which you can use to grow water plants like water hyacinth. This creates an excellent natural filter for your pond. A basin at the very end of the stream will act as a garbage collector, and it will help keep your pond cleaner.

Is it natural or man-made? Having grass grow right to the edge of your pond gives a natural appearance.

Drains

The biggest mistake pond builder's make, in my opinion,

is to leave out drains. You will find it so much easier to clean up your pond if you can just drain out the gunk. This means you need a drain wherever gunk will collect. Great places for filters are at the bottom of the pond, in filters, and in basins. It is also best have a drain with a good-sized opening of at least an inch and a half. To clean up, just open your drains and swoosh the gunk away.

Liners

You definitely want to purchase your liner before you begin digging. The problem with buying liner for a stream project is that you may have to buy more liner than you will need for the project due to the width of the liner roll. You can piece together smaller pieces of liner to be more economical, but use the pieces carefully.

Plants and a small statue add flair to this stream. Wakoola Water gardens.

Preparing Your Site

The first step in building your stream is the site excavation. First, set up your "perspective lines" if you are using this method. Remove the top layer of grass and soil. You can cut into your landscape as you move down the stream to create "steps" and "basins." Your landscape could actually be quite

Part 2

flat. Excavating a gentle slope toward your pond will give enough "oomph" for the water to get moving.

You can use a basin or waterfall-type filter as the start of your stream. It will look best if you bury most of it in the ground. You should reduce the amount of rainwater that will flow into your stream; a slight lip of soil on

Basins are used to drop streams to lower elevations. Wakoola Water gardens.

each side of the waterfall will keep the runoff from your yard from entering it. Rainwater can drag soil and lawn chemicals into your pond. This is hazardous because it will eventually fill up your stream, and lawn fertilizer will promote algae growth.

Remove all excess soil from your site and sharpen up any edges of your fall to suit your design. You can also dig in any depressions for intermediate basins at this time. You will now be ready to lay down your liner. Using a shovel will give you the best control during your excavation.

Suffering a heavy rainfall before you have put the liner down can erode your design and potentially drag a lot of mud into your pond when you add a stream. If you are using a basin at the bottom of

How to Begin

You can begin a stream without a basin at the top. You should carefully place your outlet tubing so that water does not splash out of the stream. You could cover a length of tubing with boulders, being careful not to block the opening. This will give the illusion that the water is bubbling out of the ground at the head of your stream.

the stream, you can install it temporarily to catch any mud. However, take this precaution only if you think you will have to take time between the excavation and the liner placement.

Top Basin and Plumbing

Your next step is to place the top basin, if you are using one. First get your plumbing installed into the basin. You will have tubing or pipe that will connect the basin to your pump and possibly a drain for the basin. You can also place your tubing down the side of the stream at this time. You can bury it or place it where you will be covering it with rocks and landscaping materials. Don't put the tubing under the stream itself. You may want to be able to access it later.

I recommend a "T" in the line to your stream. This gives you flexibility to adjust the flow rate to the stream or even turn the stream completely off while still running the pump.

Liner Installation

Placing your liner should not be too difficult. You will simply drape your excavation with the liner, carefully push the liner into place over any built-in steps and basins, and then work the liner into corners and

Part 2

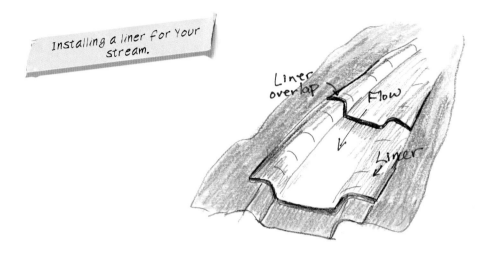

Installing a liner for your stream.

Liner overlap

Flow

Liner

contours. Don't worry about small folds in the liner where you must crease it to get a fit. You will be covering all of it with rocks later.

You can work top to bottom if you only have one piece of liner material. However, if you are using multiple pieces of liner you *must* work from the bottom to the top. Place the pieces of liner so that the piece that is higher on the hill laps over the top of the liner below it. Make sure that the first (bottom-most) piece laps into your pond or pool. It is also a good idea to run a bead of silicone sealer under the flaps where they join.

On the outer edge of your stream, create a lip of soil to contain and guide the water. You want the liner to extend beyond the watercourse 6 inches to a foot. Think about water and how it flows.

Finishing your stream with rock and gravel.

You want it to stay inside your stream. Finding out that the stream leaks later can ruin your efforts.

Rock Placement

The next task is the most interesting and possibly the hardest part of the job–rock placement. Your best artistic skills will be needed to place your stones to create a natural and realistic arrangement. Use a variety of sizes in different positions to make the arrangement look more random. Place your stones carefully and look at each one as you place it. If it doesn't seem right in a certain place, move it.

After you have placed the large stones, use gravel to fill in between rocks and cover places where the liner is showing. The gravel looks more natural than bare liner and will provide surface area for biological filtration.

There is really no need to use mortar or foam to seal your rocks in place with a stream. In a waterfall, you do this to direct the flow of water over the top of the stones. With a stream, this is really not a problem.

Wet Test

When you have everything put together and you feel that it is all perfect, start up your pump. If you have been

Large rocks and plants are used to create a natural scene.

careful, everything should work just fine. You will probably have to add water to your pond as the basins of your stream fill up. If you notice that the level of your pond falls, you may, unfortunately, have a leak in your new stream. Look for wet places in the surrounding landscape–a liner leak may show up nearby. You can adjust your rocks while the pump is running to fix any places where the water is splashing out. You will lose some water to evaporation, but you probably will not see your pond level drop over a 24-hour period due to evaporation alone.

Caring for Your Waterfall and Stream

Your waterfall shouldn't require as much daily maintenance once it is set up, but there are still a few tasks for you to do in order to keep it working well year after year. If you neglect your chores, you could have a waterfall that clogs up or begins to leak.

Algae and Pond Problems

Many waterfall problems are

A continuous flow of fresh water keeps a natural stream clean.

really pond problems. Green water is probably the most common problem with pond water, and there are many ways to tackle a green water problem. Usually, you can work with your pond to end algae blooms. Consider purchasing an ultraviolet water clarifier. The UV light kills the free-floating algae that cause the green water.

General Care

You should remove debris from your waterfall periodically. Large debris like leaves and twigs should be removed regularly. The leaves can leach tannins into the water and turn it a brown color. Don't worry–this will not be harmful to your fish or plants in the pond. It's just not very pretty. There are two ways to get rid of the color. The easiest is to get rid of the source (leaves) and do several water changes over the next several weeks. You can also try adding some activated carbon to your filter box, but it may take more carbon than is cost effective.

Mosses and marginal plants use nutrients that may otherwise cause dangerous algae blooms.

Spring and Fall

Spring and fall are good times to clean the debris from your waterfall. You can do a good job of removing leaves with a blower, and you should also go back and pick out all of the strays that are still between the rocks. Give your kids some extra allowance to spend some time leaf hunting.

After you have removed the leaves, remove any debris from your water plants. Dead and faded water plants can also add to the "browning" of your water. Most water plants can handle a pretty hard pruning, and many will die back to the roots in the fall anyway.

Finally, get ready to rinse out the mulch that has accumulated between the rocks. A good spray nozzle on your garden hose will usually do a great job. You will really

Waterfalls such as these can be dangerous to work with so always use caution when you are stepping on wet rocks.

appreciate having a drain and a basin in your waterfall at this point. Just start at the top of the fall and begin spraying the rock, forcing the debris down the stream or waterfall. Soon, most of it will be washed into your basin and out the drain. If you do not have a drain, you can place a submersible pump in the lower part of the falls and let it pump the dirty water away from your pond.

In the spring you can add some floating plants along the edge of the waterfall or stream. Parrots feather (*Myriophyllum aquaticum*) will spread out gracefully along the rocks. Small pots of other marginal plants like sweet flag, water iris, and horsetail can be tucked into your stream for variety.

Winter

In most cases, you will not be running your waterfall or stream in the winter. Unless you live in a warm climate, I recommend that you do not run the waterfall. However, there is a school of thought that by running the waterfall, you will more easily keep a hole open in the ice for your hibernating fish. Depending on your climate, you risk draining down the pond as the ice freezes in the waterfall or stream. You also will save electricity by shutting it down in the winter. Most pond-supply outlets sell small heaters designed to keep a hole open in the ice. Choose the method that you feel most comfortable with for winter.

Pennywort grows in this slow-moving stream. Wakoola Water gardens.

Summer

Summer is the best time for enjoying your waterfall or stream. There really should not be too many chores for you this time of year, as all the leaves usually remain on the trees and shrubs. Just be sure to check on things periodically, removing the odd leaf or two that blew in from a passing thunderstorm, and sit back. Enjoy those warm summer nights listening to the frogs and insects in and around your pond.

Resources

Tropical Fish Hobbyist

The leading aquarium keeping magazine, *Tropical Fish Hobbyist* has been the source of accurate, up-to-the minute, fascinating information on every facet of the aquarium hobby including freshwater fish, aquatic plants, marine aquaria, mini-reefs, and ponds for over 50 years. *TFH* will take you to new heights with its informative articles and stunning photos. With thousands of fish, plants, and other underwater creatures available, the hobbyist needs levelheaded advice about their care, maintenance, and breeding. *TFH* authors have the knowledge and experience to help make your aquarium sensational.

Tropical Fish Hobbyist
P.O. Box 427
Neptune, NJ 07754-9989

For subscription information please e-mail:
info@tfh.com
or call:
1-888-859-9034

Piedmont Koi & Watergarden Society
Geoffrey Huntley - President
E-Mail: president@remove.pkwsonline.com

Wakoola Water Gardens
5235 Union Hill Road
Cumming, GA 30040
www.wakoola.com

Index

Photo Credits

Anita Nelson: p. 102

All other photos by Terry Anne Barber.

Cartoons by Michael Pifer.

Illustrations by Terry Anne Barber.